BIBLE ACTIVITY BOOK

EASTER STORY

LEENA LANE AND ANNA TODD

Jesus enters Jerusalem

Jesus and his friends were near Jerusalem.

"Get a donkey from the village over there," said Jesus, pointing to some houses nearby. "If anyone asks you what you are doing, tell them that the Lord needs it."

They got the donkey and Jesus rode on its back into the busy city.

Many people cheered when they saw Jesus. Some threw their cloaks on the road as he passed. Others cut palm branches off the trees and spread them on the road. Everybody waved and cheered.

"The King is coming!" they shouted. "Hosanna! Praise God!"

Talk about

Talk about sharing excitement. What kinds of things get you excited? Ask someone else what they're excited about.

① ② ③ ④ ⑤

Can you see four more children in the crowd?
Draw an arrow to and put a circle around each one.

J A F C L O A K P P U T
B A P A L K L G S A K H
F J E S U S S P L L I E
J S S D O N K E Y M N R
D E J T S F Y M C K G A

Can you find the words JESUS, DONKEY, PALM, KING, and CLOAK?
Trace over the letters in another color so they stand out.

Connect the dots to see the animal Jesus rode into Jerusalem.

3

Jesus gets angry

When Jesus and his friends arrived in Jerusalem, they went to the Temple. When they got there, they found moneychangers who were cheating people who were coming to worship God. Jesus got angry and exclaimed, "God wants this to be a house of prayer, not a den of thieves!"

Talk about

Talk about anger. Anger is a feeling; it isn't right or wrong. Jesus got angry because the moneychangers were cheating people and were disrespectful to God. Jesus was right to be angry. There are still things in our world that are unjust. Ask your family about them. What can you do to help?

Can you connect each broken jar? Draw a line from each jar top to the matching bottom.

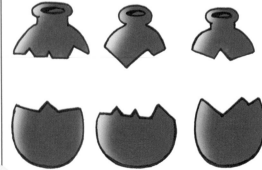

Can you find two coins that look the same? Draw a line to connect them.

Look at these pictures.

Can you find these things in the big picture? Draw a circle around them if you can.

Can you find where these five details belong in the big picture?

Write the number of each shape in the correct space in the big picture.

1

2

3

4

5

5

The story of the ten bridesmaids

Jesus told his friends a story to show them how to be ready for God's kingdom:

"Once there was a wedding. Ten bridesmaids picked up their oil lamps and went to meet the groom. Five of the bridesmaids were wise and took extra oil for their lamps. But the other five were foolish and didn't take any extra oil.

"The groom arrived late, so the bridesmaids had to wait a long time. They fell asleep.

Put a circle around the full oil lamps and draw a square around the empty ones.

How many lamps are there altogether? Write the number in the box.

"Suddenly there was a shout: 'The bridegroom is coming!' All the girls woke up.

"By now the oil in their lamps had run out. The five wise bridesmaids put their extra oil in their lamps and the lamps burned brightly. But the five foolish ones had to go and buy more oil.

"While the foolish bridesmaids were away, the groom arrived. They missed him because they were not ready."

Can you finish coloring in the people in the story?

Jesus washes his friends' feet

Can you find the mistake in this picture? Draw a circle around it.

Talk about

Talk about serving others. Remember a time when someone did something for you. What can you do today for someone else?

Jesus and his friends gathered for a special meal. He knew that it would be their last meal together before he died.

Before they sat down to eat, Jesus tied a towel round his waist. He poured some water into a bowl. Then he started to wash his friends' hot, dusty feet.

"What are you doing?" asked Peter. "I won't let you wash my feet! You are my master, not my servant!"

"Let me wash your feet," said Jesus.

At last Peter agreed.

Then Jesus said, "I have washed your feet. Now you should wash one another's feet. Look after each other as I am caring for you."

Follow the footprints to see whose feet were dirty, whose feet were clean and who was wearing shoes.
Draw the right footprints in each box.

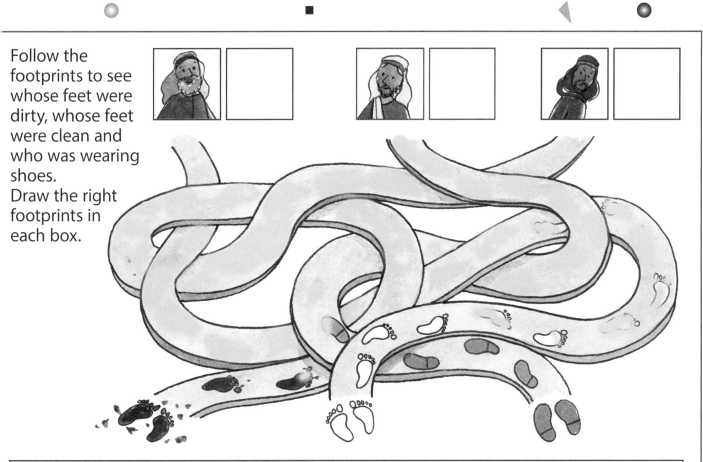

These feet appear on another page in this book.
Who do they belong to and which page are they on?

Name	Page

Can you help these three people find their own shoes?

From each pair of feet draw a line to the right size shoes.

Write a "b" in the box under the biggest feet.

Write an "s" in the box under the smallest feet.

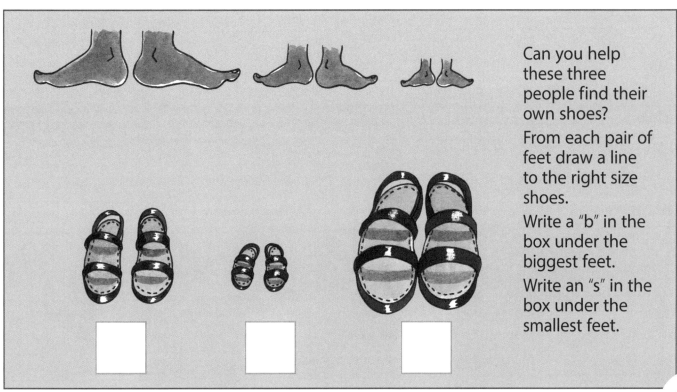

The Last Supper

On Thursday, Jesus sat down with his friends to eat a special meal. It was Passover, the time when God's people remember how God saved Moses and the Israelites from slavery in Egypt.

Jesus told his friends that he was about to die, but he wanted to give them a new way to be with him. Jesus took the bread and gave thanks to God. He broke the bread, gave it to his friends, and said, "Take this and eat it. This is my Body given up for you."

Look carefully at these things connected with the Last Supper Jesus ate. Put your hand over the picture and see how many you can remember.

Then Jesus took a cup of wine, gave thanks to God, and passed it around. He said, "Take this and drink it. This is my Blood that is poured out for the forgiveness of sins. Do this to remember me."

All Jesus' friends ate and drank. But Judas left the meal early. Judas had met with Jesus' enemies, and decided to betray him.

Finish coloring in the picture of the Last Supper.

Talk about gathering around a table for a family meal. What is it like when everyone is talking and sharing together? Did you know that the altar at church is the Lord's table? There, God's family gathers for the most special meal of all! It is a meal where Jesus continues to give us his Body and Blood. Thank God for this amazing gift!

Talk about

Count how many of Jesus' friends are sitting with him at the table and put the number in the box. Draw a circle around Judas.

Write the number of plates you can see on the table.

How many loaves of bread are there on the table?

There are not enough oranges for everyone on the table. How many of the people at the table will not be able to have one?

Jesus prays in the garden

After the meal, Jesus left the house and went to the Mount of Olives with his friends. He wanted to pray to God in the Garden of Gethsemane. He asked his friends to pray too.

Then he went a short distance away to be alone.

Jesus prayed, "Father, please help me. I want to do your will, and not my own. Give me the courage I need."

When Jesus went back to his friends, they had fallen asleep. He said to them, "How can you sleep now? Get up and pray with me!"

Then Judas, who had been one of Jesus' twelve friends, came to the garden. He brought soldiers with him. Judas betrayed Jesus, and the soldiers arrested Jesus and took him away.

Jesus' friends were frightened and ran away.

Talk about
Talk about prayer. Sometimes it's hard to pray. Can you think of a time when you found praying difficult? It doesn't matter what we are going through, God wants to be with us all the time. We can pray when we are happy or sad, confident or scared, calm or angry. Write your own prayer.

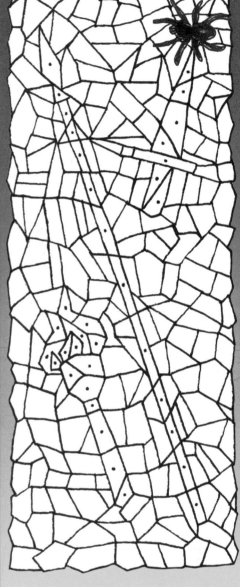

Shade in the dotted parts of the picture to see what the soldiers brought with them.

Count how many friends are running away and write the number here.

Which of these five things would you run away from?
Draw a circle round them.

Some people
are afraid of
spiders.

Can you find
seven more
spiders hiding
on these pages?

Peter lets Jesus down

At the Last Supper, Jesus warned his friend Peter about what was going to happen. "Before the rooster crows twice, you will say that you don't even know me—three times!"

After the soldiers had arrested Jesus, Peter followed them at a distance. Jesus was taken to the house of the High Priest. Peter warmed himself at the fire outside. A servant girl saw Peter and said, "Look! This is one of Jesus' friends!"

"No, I'm not! I don't even know him," Peter replied. He heard the rooster crow.

Talk about

Talk about doing the right thing. Peter denied knowing Jesus because he was afraid he might be arrested too. Can you think of a time when it was hard to do the right thing? Talk to someone in your family about why it's important to do the right thing even when it's hard.

Color in this picture of the crowing rooster.

Use the coloring guide below to help you.

Other people who were there also asked Peter about being friends with Jesus. Two more times Peter denied it.

Suddenly, the rooster crowed again. Then, Peter remembered what Jesus had told him during the Last Supper. He felt so terrible that he went away from the High Priest's house and cried.

1

2

3

4

5

Jesus on trial

Jesus was brought before the Roman governor named Pontius Pilate.

"What has this man done wrong?" asked Pilate.

"He is causing trouble all over the country," said the chief priests. "He says he is a king."

"Are you the king of the Jews?" asked Pilate.

"Yes," said Jesus.

"What do you want me to do with Jesus?" Pilate asked the crowd.

"Kill him," they shouted.

Pilate handed Jesus over to the soldiers to be whipped. But the crowd became even angrier. Then Pilate sentenced Jesus to death.

The soldiers put a purple robe on Jesus, and placed a crown of thorns on his head.

The crowd mocked him as he was led away.

Three of these soldiers were on duty at the trial.
Draw a circle round the one who was not there.

Can you find three things that should not be in the big picture?

The Romans didn't use numbers like we do. They used letters like this:

$$I = 1$$
$$V = 5$$
$$X = 10$$

How many Roman soldiers are there in the big picture? Write your answer in Roman letters.

How many people are there behind the soldiers? Write your answer in Roman letters.

Write the answer to this sum:

$$V + V =$$

What is this figure in numbers?

$$XVI$$

Talk about Talk about suffering. Jesus did not deserve to suffer. Sometimes bad things happen which hurt people. Ask God to be with all the people who are suffering.

Write the name of this object here.

_____

Write the name of the man it was made for.

_____

Jesus dies on the cross

On Friday, Jesus was taken to a place on a hill called Golgotha. There he was crucified between two robbers. Jesus had done nothing wrong.

Jesus' friend John, his friend Mary Magdalene, and his mother, Mary, stood beneath the cross. Even though Jesus was in a lot of pain he continued to love and

There were three crosses on the hill that terrible day. Can you mark three cross shapes in the box?

forgive others. While hanging on the cross he cried out to God, "Father, forgive them. They don't know what they are doing."

Darkness covered the land, and Jesus died. His body was taken down from the cross and given to a man named Joseph of Arimethea. He put Jesus' body in a tomb. Then a large stone was rolled in front of the entrance to the tomb.

Talk about

Talk about hope. Hope is knowing that God is there for us and will save us even when it seems that things couldn't be worse. Share a story of hope with a family member or friend.

Can you connect all the dots using twelve lines to form a cross?

Where has Jesus gone?

Saturday was a day of rest. Early on Sunday morning, Mary Magdalene and some other women went to the tomb. They came to anoint Jesus' body. When they got there, the large stone had been rolled away. The tomb was empty!

Jesus' body was gone. All that was left was the cloth that had covered him. What happened?

The garden is full of fruit trees and grapevines.

How many of the following can you find in the big picture?

Palm trees

Olive trees

Grape bunches

Fig trees

Can you find all the differences between these two pictures? Draw a line to point to each difference.
One has been done. There are nine more to find.

1 2 3 4 5 6 7 8 9 10

Angels

Mary Magdalene and her friends were very surprised to find that Jesus' body was gone. Who could have rolled the big stone away? It was very heavy.

Suddenly, two angels in bright, shining clothes appeared.

"Why are you looking for Jesus here?" they asked the women. "He is not dead. He is alive again!"

The women were amazed and ran off to tell all Jesus' friends what had happened.

Talk about surprises. We can be surprised by something good or bad. The women who went to the tomb that Sunday morning received amazing news. Jesus' resurrection is the best surprise of all! How can you share the good news of Easter with someone today?

Talk abo

Mary Magdalene ran to tell her friends the good news.
Follow the paths to help her find the right road to the village.

The stone was very heavy.

Can you sort all the objects in order of weight? Write number 1 under the lightest object and number 7 under the heaviest.

Jesus is alive!

Jesus is
_____

Outside the tomb, Mary Magdalene cried. She missed Jesus and still wondered where he was. Suddenly, Mary heard a voice. She turned around and saw a man who looked like a gardener. "Mary," the man said.

Then Mary knew who the man was. It was Jesus!

Mary Magdalene ran off to tell everyone the amazing news. "Jesus died, but now he is risen from the dead. I have seen the Lord!"

Write down how many of each of the following things you can find in the picture.

Jesus appears to his friends

Two of Jesus' friends were on their way to a village called Emmaus, near Jerusalem. They talked a lot about Jesus.

A little while later, another man came and walked alongside them. They didn't know who he was. He asked them lots of questions about Jesus. The two friends

Talk about meeting God. The two friends met Jesus on the road, but they didn't recognize him. God is with us in many ways too, but we don't always realize it. Look for three ways God was with you today.

Talk about

told him how Jesus had died on a cross, how he had been put in the tomb, and how the women had found the tomb empty.

As they came near to Emmaus, the two friends asked the man to come and eat with them. The man sat down and picked up some bread. He broke it into smaller pieces and thanked God for it.

Suddenly they knew who this man was—it was Jesus! He was alive!

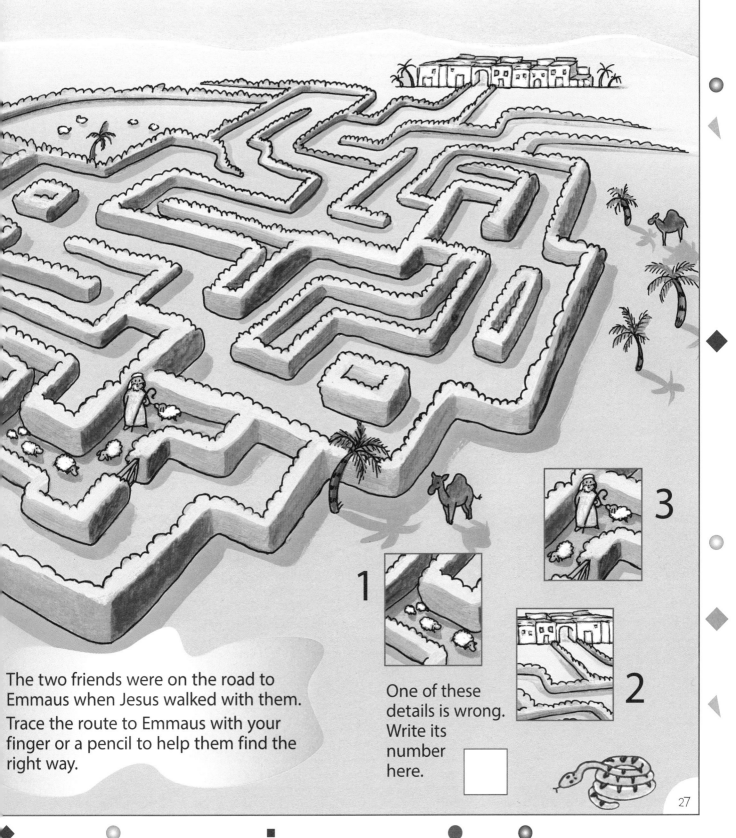

The two friends were on the road to Emmaus when Jesus walked with them.

Trace the route to Emmaus with your finger or a pencil to help them find the right way.

One of these details is wrong. Write its number here.

Thomas

Thomas was one of Jesus' friends. When the others told him that Jesus was alive, Thomas didn't believe it.

"He can't be," said Thomas. "It's impossible."

"But we've seen Jesus!" said the other friends.

"Well," said Thomas, "I won't believe Jesus is alive unless I see the wounds in his hands and feet."

A week later, Jesus came to see all his friends. Jesus said to Thomas, "Look at my hands and feet, Thomas. Now do you believe it is me—your friend Jesus?"

Thomas knew at once that it was Jesus.

"You believe now that you have seen me," said Jesus. "But there will be many people who will believe in me without seeing."

Talk about

Talk about seeing and believing. We all know that there are things we cannot see. Some examples are the wind, love, and atoms. God is also real. We don't have to see him to experience his love. Ask God to help you believe in him even though you can't see him.

Who was the first person to see Jesus alive again?

How many days did Thomas have to wait to see Jesus for himself?

Connect the dots to see what
Jesus showed Thomas.
You can color in the picture.

Thomas could not
believe that it was
really Jesus.

Can you recognize
which of these
pictures is Jesus?
Check the two
pictures that are of
Jesus and put an "x"
under the three
pictures that are not
Jesus.

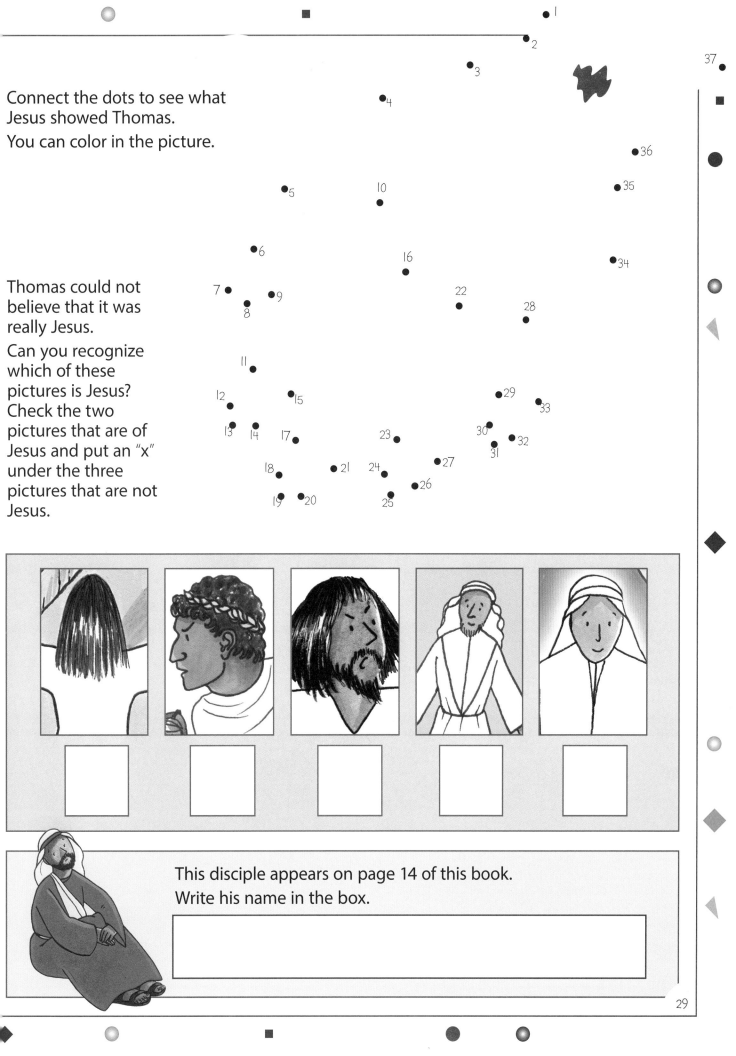

This disciple appears on page 14 of this book.
Write his name in the box.

Jesus cooks breakfast on the beach

Jesus appeared once more to his friends on the shores of the Sea of Galilee. Peter, Thomas, and Jesus' other friends were fishing on the lake. They had tried to catch fish all night, but hadn't caught a thing.

A man called from the shore, "Throw your net on the other side of the boat and you will catch lots of fish!"

The friends did as he said and suddenly the net was filled with so many fish that they could hardly hold on to it!

Peter knew at once who the man on the shore was. It was Jesus! Peter jumped into the water and swam to shore. Jesus was on the beach cooking fish. They all ate together. It was so good to see Jesus again!

There are five different kinds of fish in the net.

Color each kind a different color.

Write down the number of each type of fish in the boxes.

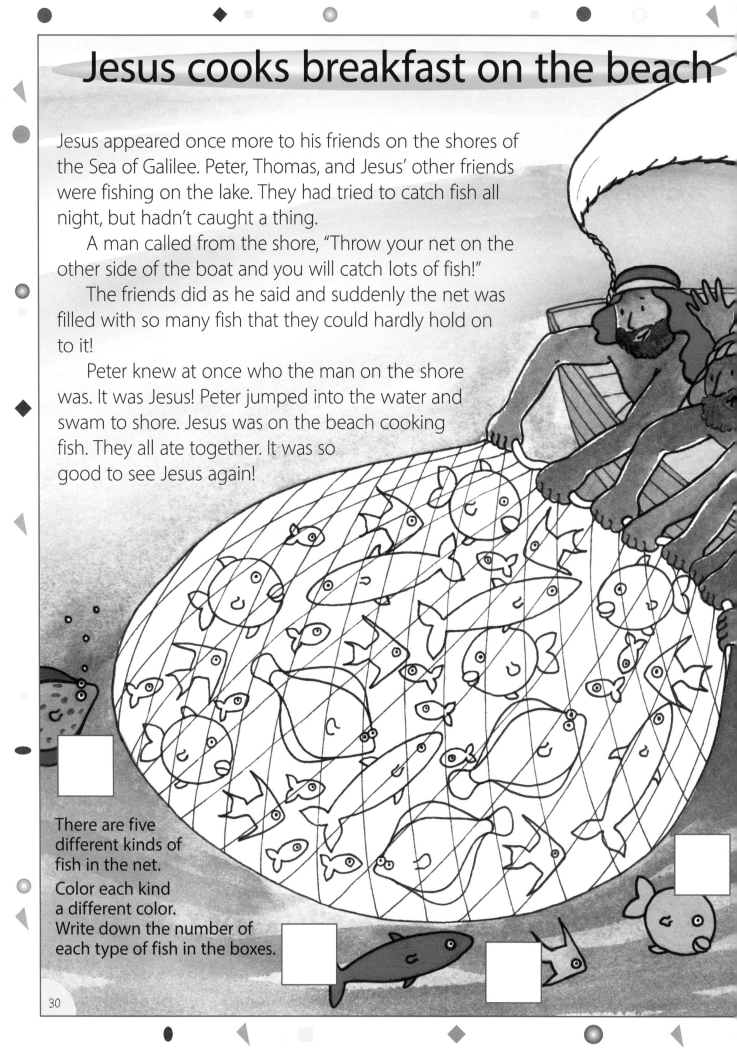

How many of Jesus' friends are fishing in the boat?

Here are two pictures of Jesus cooking fish on the beach.

Can you find six differences between them? Draw a line from the number to each difference on this picture.

① ② ③ ④ ⑤ ⑥

Talk about

Talk about how Jesus' story never ends. Jesus appeared to many of his friends after he had risen from the dead. Forty days later, he went back up to heaven on a cloud. As Jesus was ascending, he said, "Go, and tell everyone the Good News! I am going to make a home in heaven for you. But, I am with you always, even until the end of time!" Tell the story of Easter to someone you love. Pray for everyone who has not yet heard the Good News.

ISBN-10: 0-8198-2397-X
ISBN-13: 978-0-8198-2397-7

"P" and PAULINE are registered trademarks of the Daughters of St. Paul.
First North American edition
Published by Pauline Books & Media, 50 Saint Paul's Avenue, Boston, MA 02130-3491
Copyright © Anno Domini Publishing, Leena Lane Author, Roma Bishop Illustrator.
Printed in Singapore
EDBAB TLPLHK5555554-27100004 2397-X
www.pauline.org
Pauline Books & Media is the publishing house of the Daughters of St. Paul, an international congregation of women religious serving the Church with the communications media.

1 2 3 4 5 6 7 8 9   19 18 17 16 15

Can you can find all these animals in the book?
Write the page numbers on which the animals appear in the red boxes.

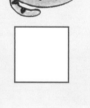